BAPTISM

BAPTISM

JACK HAY

40 Beansburn, Kilmarnock, Scotland

ISBN-13: 978 1 904064 97 8
ISBN-10: 1 904064 97 3

Copyright © 2010 by John Ritchie Ltd.
40 Beansburn, Kilmarnock, Scotland

All rights reserved. No part of this publication may be reproduced, stored in a retrievable system, or transmitted in any form or by any other means – electronic, mechanical, photocopy, recording or otherwise – without prior permission of the copyright owner.

Typeset by John Ritchie Ltd., Kilmarnock
Printed by Bell & Bain Ltd., Glasgow

Contents

Preface 7
Introduction 9
The Command 11
The Method 14
The Participants 16
The Timing 20
The Significance 21
The Practicalities 23
Conclusion 24
Appendix 1. Romans ch.6 25
Appendix 2. 1 Peter 3.21 27
Appendix 3. Acts 2.38; ch.22.16 28
Appendix 4. Children 29
Appendix 5. 1 Corinthians 1.13-17 30
Appendix 6. "Baptized for the Dead". 1 Corinthians 15.29 30

Preface

The main purpose of this booklet is to set out in simple terms what the Bible teaches about Christian baptism. The major part of the presentation is intended to be a help to people who have begun to take an interest in the Scriptures, or who have perhaps recently come to know the Lord Jesus as Saviour and Lord. It will be explained from the New Testament that one of the next steps on the pathway of faith is baptism.

For believers who have been on the Christian road a little longer, appendices have been added to deal with some of the more complicated aspects of the subject.

Baptism

INTRODUCTION

In the Old Testament, the religious life of the people of Israel involved a tremendous range of rituals and ceremonies. There was legislation that covered even the ordinary affairs of life such as diet and dress. By contrast, New Testament Christianity is uncomplicated, and there are only two ordinances associated with it. The one is baptism and the other the Lord's Supper, more commonly described in the Bible as the breaking of bread. There are a few similarities between these two ordinances and these are considered below.

• The Lord Jesus commanded both of them before He went back to heaven. On the eve of His crucifixion while celebrating the Feast of Passover, He instituted **the Lord's Supper.** He took a loaf and likened it to His body, and a cup which He likened to His blood. The command was to eat and drink in remembrance of Him (Luke 22.19-20). Before His ascension He commissioned His apostles to go out and preach, and to **baptise** the converts (Matthew 28.18-20). So then, being baptised and participating in the Lord's Supper are both acts of obedience to the commands of Christ.

• According to the Acts of the Apostles the early Christians practised both of these ordinances. As far as **the breaking of bread** is concerned, there is clear indication of *who* should participate (Acts 2.41-42). In Acts 20.7, the emphasis is on *when* the ordinance should be celebrated. The numerous references to **baptism** in the Book of Acts will be examined later in the booklet.

• Paul explained both of the ordinances in the epistles. **Baptism** is dealt with in Romans ch.6, another passage that will feature in this booklet. **The Lord's Supper** features in 1 Corinthians 11.23-34. As at the institution of the Supper, stress is laid on the fact that it is an act of remembrance, with the added disclosure that as often as it is done, there is a proclamation of the Lord's death (v.26). To whom is this proclamation made? Visitors could be there to observe proceedings (1 Corinthians 14.23-25) and angels are certainly in attendance (ch.11.10). That is one of the reasons that Paul advances for the sisters having their heads covered in the gatherings of a local New Testament church. These interested angels are looking on, and for their eyes, the order of headship should be in place in the local church not only in reality but also in symbol, in that brothers will meet with uncovered heads, and sisters with their heads covered. To all these interested parties then, human and angelic, the eating and drinking is a kind of visual aid of the events of Calvary.

Thus there are these comparisons between the two ordinances, but they end there. Consider now some contrasting features between the two ordinances.

• **Baptism** is a once-in-a-lifetime experience whereas **the Lord's Supper** is observed at regular intervals. *"As often* as ye eat this bread and drink this cup, ye do shew the Lord's death till he come" (1 Corinthians 11.26). The Lord's Supper will be observed habitually until the Lord Jesus comes again.

• **Baptism** is a personal activity, but **the Lord's Supper** is a congregational activity of New Testament churches. ("New Testament churches" are gatherings of Christians who try to function collectively in the same way as believers did in New Testament times. The New Testament calls them "churches of God"). The breaking of bread was never observed in isolation or independent of the local church.

- In **baptism** a believer is identified with Christ in His death (Romans 6.3). In **the Lord's Supper** as has been noted, there is a proclamation of His death; "as often as ye eat this bread, and drink this cup, *ye do shew the Lord's death* till he come" (1 Corinthians 11.26).

THE COMMAND

The command to baptise was given by the Lord Jesus Christ Himself when He commissioned His apostles to preach the gospel. "Go ye therefore, and teach all nations, **baptizing them** in the name of the Father, and of the Son, and of the Holy Ghost" (Matthew 28.19). Their remit was to evangelise, and they were under orders to baptise the people who believed the message that they carried. These instructions were followed implicitly as is clear from even a casual reading of the book of Acts. For example, the preaching convicted Peter's audience and they asked, "What shall we do"? They were told "Repent, and **be baptized**" (Act 2.37-38). Of Cornelius and his fellow converts the Bible says, Peter "**commanded** them to be baptized in the name of the Lord" (Acts 10.48). In obedience to the Lord's command then, these early preachers insisted on the need for baptism.

This prompts the question; "Is baptism really essential"? It is certainly not essential for the salvation of the soul. Large areas of the New Testament are devoted to showing that salvation is by the grace of God, and is based entirely on the death and resurrection of the Lord Jesus. It is received by faith in Him alone with no additions necessary. "Believe on the Lord Jesus Christ, and thou shalt be saved" (Acts 16.31). "Whosoever shall call upon the name of the Lord shall be saved" (Romans 10.13). "By grace are ye saved through faith" (Ephesians 2.8). That is the starting point of the spiritual journey that leads to heaven. Have you embarked on that journey? Have you stepped out on the narrow way that leads to life? (Matthew 7.13-14).

As we shall observe, in the New Testament submitting to baptism was always a step subsequent to the conversion experience, so there is no point in giving it serious consideration without first attending to the matter of your soul's salvation. That is the priority, and baptism will not achieve it. In the Bible there is no such thing as baptismal regeneration as is taught in some religious circles. Nowhere in the Bible is there ever the suggestion that baptism in any way makes a person a member of Christ and an inheritor of His kingdom. It is never seen as a so-called "means of grace". Being born again is dependent on receiving Christ, that is, believing on Him (John 1.12-13). Have you ever received Him?

It is crucial to be able to look back to that great decision that transforms the life and changes the destiny for eternity. I ask again then, have you ever received Christ? If not, take stock of your position. According to the Bible's teaching, as things stand, you are still estranged from God because of unforgiven sin. Were you to die, that situation would become irreversible, meaning that you would be lost for eternity. But God has loved you and provided salvation through the death and resurrection of the Lord Jesus Christ. That salvation can be yours by repentance and faith on your part. Take the step of calling on Him for His great salvation, for "whosoever believeth on him shall receive the remission of sins" (Acts 10.43).

The Command

In addressing the question, "Is baptism essential" we state emphatically then that as far as salvation is concerned the answer is a definite "no". The Lord Jesus promised the repentant thief who was hanging at His side that he would be with Him in paradise, and there was no opportunity for that dying criminal to submit to the ordinance of baptism (Luke 23.39-43); there will be unbaptised believers in heaven. Tragically, in hell there will be many who have been baptised, but who were relying on their baptism or other religious activities for salvation, rather than on the Lord Jesus Christ who died and rose again.

While baptism does not contribute to salvation, there is another sense in which it is absolutely essential. We have noted that to be baptised was **a command** from the Lord. If you have been saved, you will remember that in your unconverted days you had no inclination to obey Him. You were among those whom Paul described as "children of disobedience" (Ephesians 2.2). Now your status has been changed, and you are among those whom Peter called "obedient children" (1 Peter 1.14). For the Christian, obedience to Christ is not an option. For those who profess to love Him, compliance with His demands gives proof of that affection. He said, "If ye love me, keep my commandments" (John 14.15). It also gives the personal assurance of a genuine conversion to Christ. "Hereby we do know that we know him, if we keep his commandments" (1 John 2.3). God always set great store on obedience. In Old Testament days He valued it above all the ritual of the ancient sacrificial system of worship. "To obey is better than sacrifice" (1 Samuel 15.22). Even today obedience is far more important than any profession of commitment that falls glibly from the lips. "Why call ye me, Lord, Lord, and do not the things which I say"? (Luke 6.46). Among other things then, baptism is an act of obedience on the part of the believer; while it is not necessary for salvation, it is a vital step as far as a life of obedience is concerned. Have you obeyed the command? If not, in consecration bring your will into line with His, and prove that His will is "good, and acceptable, and perfect" (Romans 12.2). Peter described baptism as "the answer of a good conscience toward God" (1 Peter 3.21).

THE METHOD

It is generally known that among what are called Christian denominations there are two distinct methods of administering the ordinance of baptism. The most widely practised is commonly called "christening", and involves sprinkling some water on the head of the participant, in most cases an infant. The second seems more complicated, and requires a depth of water, for the person involved is briefly immersed in the water and hence the term, "baptism by immersion". From a biblical standpoint, which of these is the correct method? Both cannot be right, so we must get back to the Bible to discover what it has to say about this important subject; we take our guidance from Scripture and not from church tradition. If you have discovered already that to be baptised is a command that you must obey, I am sure that you want to obey it in the proper scriptural way. The Bible was the book that revealed to you how to be saved (2 Timothy 3.15). Now that you are a Christian it is that same book that explains the next step, and indeed, it provides guidance for every aspect of your life.

In a number of ways, the New Testament Scriptures show that the mode of baptism should be by immersion in water.

• The word *baptise* is a word that has been absorbed into English from the Greek language, and the basic meaning of the Greek word is to dip. It is the word that a Greek woman would have used when she was dyeing a garment. She would have "baptised" the item in the basin of dye. It is the word that the lady would have used when pickling her vegetables. She "baptised" them in the vinegar solution. Pouring the solution over them would have been pointless. Thus the word itself carries the concept of immersion. If early Bible translators had been true to their convictions they would have translated the word by the English word "dip". It seems that they were reluctant to offend religious convention and so they compromised by coining a new English word "baptise" taken straight from the Greek.

• When people were baptised by John the Baptist it did not carry the same significance as Christian baptism, but the form was the same. John baptised the Lord Jesus by immersion. When Mark recorded the event, he spoke of the Lord being "baptized of John *in* Jordan" (ch.1.9). He then referred to Him "coming up out of the water" (v.10). In fact, the Greek preposition *eis* translated "in" in v.9 means "into", so the Lord was baptised *into* Jordan, clearly a reference to immersion in the river. Artists have depicted the scene on the basis of religious tradition rather than the biblical record. They portray the Lord kneeling on the bank of the River Jordan with John pouring water on His head from a vial. If only they had read their Bibles before putting brush to canvas!

• The story of the conversion of an African man is recorded in Acts ch.8, and it tells of his subsequent baptism. An evangelist by the name of Philip was the preacher who brought news of Christ to the Ethiopian, and on hearing his confession of faith, Philip baptised him. Of Philip and the convert the Bible says this; "they went down both into the water". After the baptism, they came up out of the water (vv.38-39). It seems obvious from the language used that Philip had immersed the Ethiopian in a desert pool that lay along their route. Had the alternative method of baptism been in vogue or had it been scriptural, a few drops from a water bottle would have been sufficient, but clearly, the proper mode of baptism necessitated both Philip and the Ethiopian being in the water.

- It was stated earlier that Paul explained the doctrinal implications of baptism in Romans ch.6. The thought connected with it is that of burial and resurrection (vv.3-4). As believers, we died to sin the moment we trusted the Saviour, and now are expected to give evidence of new life; we walk in "newness of life". Baptism illustrates these spiritual facts, and so to express the significance of the symbolism of baptism, it has to be carried out by immersion. A sprinkling of water does not satisfy the imagery of burial and resurrection. More attention will be given to Romans ch.6 later in the booklet.

THE PARTICIPANTS

The New Testament gives clear teaching about who should be baptised. As has already been stated, those who have a preference for christening frequently "baptise" infants. Normally there is connected with the ceremony the naming of the child, and the promise on the part of parents and friends to be spiritual guardians to the young one. The impression is left that the child itself has been united to Christ and has become the recipient of spiritual blessings as a result of what has taken place. One of the most disturbing scenes in English literature is that of Tess of the D'Urbervilles christening her dying illegitimate child lest the boy should perish. It is fiction, but it reflected conventional thinking, a view that is still in place in the modern religious world.

Is there any precedent for infant baptism in the Word of God? You will search in vain to find it. A former missionary to Japan produced a pamphlet entitled "What the Bible Teaches about Infant Baptism". That title was blazoned on the front cover, but when the leaflet was opened its pages were blank! It was a novel and imaginative way of getting the point over.

The Scriptures show clearly that people who were baptised had first of all been converted to Christ; baptism is exclusively for believers. In the Acts of the Apostles there was one case of twelve men at Ephesus being baptised prior to hearing and believing the gospel of Christ. They were therefore rebaptised after they believed (Acts 19.1-7). The lesson is that anyone who has been baptised by any form of invalid baptism prior to their conversion should be baptised over again when they are saved by the grace of God. Some of you may fall into that category. Perhaps religious parents arranged your "baptism" when you were young, or maybe as a personal decision you elected to be baptised with a view to joining a church. Now that you are saved, you should think seriously about the need for baptism in the biblical way despite your past experience.

You may find that your denomination takes great exception to any thought of you being rebaptised. Its officials may quote a Bible verse to try to under-gird their opposition to your intentions. There is "one baptism" (Ephesians 4.5) they will tell you. They will deem it a serious offence for you "to go back" on your original baptism by submitting to the ordinance now that you are a Christian. It is true that there is "one baptism", but every Bible verse must be interpreted in its context. The whole background to the statement is, that people from both Jewish and Gentile backgrounds had become Christians, and both submitted to the same baptism, just as both had the same Father, and both had the same Lord etc. There was not a separate baptism for Jewish believers and Gentile believers. There was only "one baptism", but the statement does not militate against the need for being rebaptised as a believer.

Take time to examine the following references in the book of Acts. Each narrative shows that it was only after people believed on the Lord Jesus that they were baptised.

- Three thousand people who "received" Peter's message on

the Day of Pentecost were thereafter baptised (ch.2.41). Receiving his word involved among other things calling upon the name of the Lord (v.21). It involved repentance (v.38). In other words, these people had been converted to Christ. Only then were they baptised.

• Citizens of Samaria who believed Philip's preaching "were baptized, both men and women" (ch.8.12). The exponents of infant christening have been keen to make a parallel between it and Old Testament circumcision. If the alleged similarity were carried to its logical conclusion only males would be baptised. This Scripture stresses that "both men *and women* were baptized". Again though, it was only after "they believed".

• Attention has already been drawn to the Ethiopian who was saved and baptised in ch.8.

• The same pattern is followed with the conversion of Paul in ch.9. His conversion on the Damascus road was the necessary precursor to his baptism, the record of which is in v.18.

• In ch.10 the terminology that is used regarding Cornelius is rather different, but it amounts to the same thing. Before he was baptised in water he had "received the Holy Ghost" (v47-48). People receive the Holy Spirit by faith in Christ. It is not an experience subsequent to conversion. The faith that saves is the same faith that brings the Holy Spirit to reside within (Ephesians 1.13; Galatians 3.2). So Cornelius and his friends had believed, and had thus received the Holy Spirit; so having been converted, they were then baptised.

• At Philippi, it was only after Lydia's heart was opened and she received the Lord Jesus as Saviour that she was baptised (ch.16.14-15).

- In the same city, it was only after enquiry about salvation and acceptance of the message of life that a jailor in the town was baptised (ch.16.29-34). He was not told to be baptised in order to be saved. He was not told to join the religious group that met at the river in order to be saved. He was not told to reform his character and work on his cruel disposition in order to be saved. He was told to believe on the Lord Jesus Christ in order to be saved. Having done that he was then baptised.

- In a concise way, Luke the inspired writer tells of events at Corinth when the gospel was proclaimed there; "many of the Corinthians hearing believed, and were baptized" (ch.18.8). That is the precedent for our day. People must hear the message, and if they believe it, then and only then should they be baptised. Perhaps like the Corinthians you have heard and believed. Is it not time that you took a leaf out of their book by taking the next step and being baptised?

The champions for infant baptism make a lot of the fact that on three occasions in the New Testament, households were baptised. Take time to examine the three instances.

- Lydia; (Acts 16.15). There is no suggestion from Luke's pen that there were any children in Lydia's household. In fact, there is no record of her having either a husband or children. She was a businesswoman in the drapery trade, and far from home (v.14). If there has to be speculation about the make-up of her household, it would be more logical to suggest servants rather than infants. Those in her house are described in v.40 as "brethren".

- The jailor "was baptized, he and all his" (ch.16.33), so in this case it does look as if a family was involved. However, every one of them was old enough to hear the Word of God.

"They spake unto him the word of the Lord, **and to all that were in his house**" (v.32). They were also old enough to believe the message that they heard for we are told that he was "believing in God **with all his house**" (v.34). So because they were all old enough to hear, and old enough to believe, they were also old enough to be baptised.

- The third household to be baptised was that of Stephanas at Corinth (1 Corinthians 1.16). Another mention of them in that letter proves that they were not youngsters. "The house of Stephanas…they have addicted themselves to the ministry of the saints" (ch.16.15). Only those at a certain level of maturity would be in a position to serve their fellow-believers.

So then, we do have these three instances of households being baptised, but none of them provides a foundation for legitimately baptising either infants or unconverted people who may be in some way connected to the believers. The scriptural sequence is for salvation to precede baptism.

THE TIMING

In a general way, we have noted that as far as timing is concerned, baptism should be after conversion. To be more precise now, if you were to examine some of the incidents already cited, you will notice that those who were converted were baptised **immediately** after conversion. The Ethiopian did not wait until he had reached journey's end before being baptised. Having been saved in the dead of night, the jailor did not wait until the dawn, but was baptised "the same hour of the night" (ch.16.33). In fact the longest recorded gap between conversion and baptism was in the case of Paul and that was three days! Whenever the physical blindness of these three days was lifted he was baptised right away (ch.9.9,18). Although he was only three days saved a man called Ananias had challenged him, "Why tarriest thou? arise, and be baptized" (ch.22.16). How long have you been saved? If it was some time in the past, I repeat Ananias' question, "Why tarriest thou"? Or to give the Ethiopian's question a little twist, what hinders you from being baptised? (ch.8.36). For some it may be a genuine fear of water. For others it may be a fear of criticism. Some others may perceive it as a step too far in terms of loyalty to Christ. Whatever, the reason, abandon it and be willing to acknowledge the demands of your Lord, and take that step of obedience.

THE SIGNIFICANCE

Among other things, baptism is an opportunity for believers to make a public statement of their new links with Christ. Faith is something that is invisible and intangible, and one of the ways by which a believer can express his attachment to Christ is by being baptised. It is "baptism (into association with) Jesus Christ" (Romans 6.3; Galatians 3.27).

There are various ways by which believers ought to make an open acknowledgement of their links with Christ. Confessing *with the mouth* that Jesus is Lord is an integral part of the conversion experience, (Romans 10.9). The Lord does want His people to be open in their acknowledgement of Him. He warned against being "ashamed" of Him "in this adulterous and sinful generation" (Mark 8.38). The woman who touched the hem of His garment would have been content to slip away undetected, but the Lord Jesus wanted her to publicly acknowledge Him (Mark 5.25-34).

A transformed life is another powerful testimony to the power of Christ in a man's experience. In reality, a conversion that leaves no change in the life is no conversion at all. It is only an emotional religious profession with no value for eternity. While the testimony of the lip is of great value and the testimony of a changed life is equally important, **these things should be in addition to baptism and not a substitute for it**. Baptism is a very open demonstration of where our loyalties now lie.

New Testament preaching involved the insistence on baptism. In fact, believing for salvation and baptism were so closely linked that the Lord Jesus mentioned them both in the same breath when He commissioned His apostles. "He that believeth and is baptized shall be saved" (Mark 16.16). His subsequent statement leaves us in no doubt that it is the lack of faith that exposes men to the judgment of God, and not being unbaptised. However, the apostles did obey His command to preach baptism in conjunction with conversion; they were adamant that this public avowal of allegiance to Christ was so essential.

Reference has already been made to Romans 6, where the doctrine of baptism is taught. Believers have had an experience so radical as to be described as a death and resurrection. In actual fact, God regards it all as having taken place when His Son was crucified and rose again. "Our old man is crucified with him" (v.6). We are "dead with Christ" (v.8). That is the negative side of things, and among other things our association with Christ in His death has ended our servitude to the tyranny of sin. Its power over us has been broken because we died.

On the positive side, we have been associated with Christ in His resurrection, and in practical terms that means that we should "walk in newness of life" (v.4). There is a new power for living; we are "alive unto God through Jesus Christ our Lord" (v.11). These glorious facts are symbolised in baptism, so while baptism is an event that occupies one minute of a believer's life, its implications extend till death or the Lord's coming. It is so important to live in a way that expresses practically the symbolism of baptism.

Paul cites an Old Testament illustration of this when he speaks about the people of Israel being "baptized unto Moses in the cloud and in the sea" (1 Corinthians 10.2). Their "baptism" brought them into association with a new leader, Moses, and it severed their links with their old environment and their longstanding slavery. The waters of the Red Sea now lay between them and Egypt. Similarly, Christian baptism is saying in symbol that we are now linked to a new authority, Jesus as Lord, and that our slavery to sin is a thing of the past because we died to sin (Romans 6.2). Diligence should be shown daily to make the meaning of the symbol a reality in our lives.

THE PRACTICALITIES

As an author and preacher, I aim for results by looking to God to give the increase (1 Corinthians 3.6). When the gospel is preached it is right to expect a response from sinners. When the Word of God is taught, either audibly or in written form, believers who have submissive hearts will react positively. What I am saying is that I expect some readers of this booklet to want to be baptised. It could be that you are among those who feel challenged. If God has been speaking to you, and a desire to obey the Lord in this matter of baptism has been stirred within your heart, you may be wondering, "What steps should I take?"

• If you purchased the booklet in a Christian bookstore, perhaps the person who served you could direct you to someone who could take initial steps to make your desire for baptism known. If someone you know gave you the booklet, they did so in the hope that it would be helpful to you. They would no doubt have access to some facility for baptism. More likely, the Christians who brought the gospel to you and had the joy of seeing you saved have had a desire to see you take this step of progress. They would be able to arrange for you to see their elders to talk the matter through. These men will treat you courteously and kindly, so don't be anxious! The main purpose for the conversation will be for you to tell them simply about how you came to know the Lord. We have been seeing that it is only believers who should be baptised and the elders are simply safeguarding that position.

• When a suitable date has been arranged, try to circulate the details to as many of your friends as possible, because again, as noted earlier, among other things baptism is a public confession of faith in Christ. The occasion could impact on your friends, either with a view to their salvation or to them taking an interest in baptism themselves.

• Those conducting your baptism will guide you with regard to suitable clothing, and how best to carry the procedure through.

CONCLUSION

Every reader now has the responsibility to check the content of the booklet with the teaching of the Word of God, so allow me to encourage you to be like the people of Berea who "searched the scriptures daily, whether those things were so" (Acts 17.11).

One of the major points that has been made is that in the New Testament baptism was linked integrally with conversion, so it is not a passport to church fellowship. However, it is clear from Scripture that it was a necessary prerequisite for church fellowship. There is a spiritual order in Acts 2.41-42 that should not be disturbed even today. First, people received by faith what they heard that is, they were saved. Next they were baptised. Then they committed to the apostles' teaching which is now enshrined in what we call the New Testament. Subscribing to the apostles' teaching formed the basis of their fellowship, and that fellowship was expressed in the breaking of bread and prayers. That is our pattern and so we encourage every believer not to stop short, but to be willing to take every step that will bring the full enjoyment of fellowship with Christ and His people. To go back to where we started then, there are the two ordinances connected to New Testament Christianity, baptism and the Lord's Supper, and submitting to the first is a necessary stepping stone to the enjoyment of the second.

APPENDIX 1. Romans ch.6

As was stated in the introduction, Romans ch. 6 outlines Bible doctrine on the subject of baptism. The background is important. Paul had made a great declaration, "where sin abounded, grace did much more abound" (ch.5.20). He anticipated his statement being misconstrued, allowing license for sin on the premise that the more we sin, the greater the opportunity for a display of the grace of God. Indeed, there were some who actually taught that, and were "turning the grace of our God into lasciviousness" (Jude 4). Thus Paul posed the question, "Shall we continue in sin, that grace may abound?" The answer was an unequivocal "no" (Romans 6.1-2).

As part of his argument against sinful living, he contended that it would be totally inconsistent with the fact that we died to sin (v.2). When did that take place? Verse 6 supplies the answer; "our old man was crucified with (Christ), that the body of sin might be destroyed". Although we were yet to be born, God regarded us as having died to sin when the Lord Jesus was crucified. Our "old man" is all that we were in our unconverted days as descendants of Adam, and God sees that as having been finished at the cross. The present practical effect of that is that "the body of sin" has been "destroyed". The "body of sin" is the human body through which sin expressed itself. Our hands were involved in sinful actions, and our feet took us to sinful haunts and so on. Because of our association with Christ at the cross, that "body of sin" has become idle, it is reduced to inactivity, the meaning of the word translated "destroyed". The fact that we died ended our servitude to sin, and we are no longer under obligation to it. It is a legal principle that death ends all contracts. To "continue in sin" would be a denial of that principle.

On the positive side, we have not only died with Christ, but we "also live with him" (v.8), and He "liveth unto God" (v.10); hence the need to see ourselves as those who are "alive unto God" (v.11). Put simply then, our death with Christ ended the tyranny of sin in our lives, and the fact that we live with Him now places us under the authority of God as our new Master.

In the heart of all this life-changing doctrine, Paul introduced the concept of baptism (vv.3-4). This ordinance whereby the individual is momentarily immersed in water before re-emerging, clearly symbolises burial and resurrection. The spiritual teaching that Paul was about to explain is illustrated for believers at the time of their baptism. In a sense, baptism is a visual aid, a constant reminder of our death to sin, and the "newness of life" that is now a feature of our present existence. At a physical level, satisfying the significance of the symbolism requires that the method of baptism should be immersion rather than sprinkling. At a spiritual level, satisfying the symbolism requires the believer to constantly remember that he is no longer at the beck and call of the tyrant called sin; his union with Christ in His death has severed his links with that old master and there is now a new life-principle that is motivating his behaviour.

Practically, this involves a deliberate calculation on the part of the believer to lay hold on what is an accomplished fact on God's side, and so Paul says "reckon ye also yourselves to be dead indeed unto sin, but alive unto God" (v11). Baptism is a visible expression of these great spiritual truths.

APPENDIX 2. 1 Peter 3.21

A careless reading of this verse might leave the impression that baptism saves us or is at least a contributory factor in our salvation. Peter had been speaking about Noah and his family being saved through the waters of the great flood. Borne on the face of the waters they were transferred from an old order of things to a sphere that was completely new. Peter asserted that baptism carries the same imagery as the flood, "the like figure". Both are illustrative of the great work of the cross, described by the Lord Jesus as "a baptism" with which He was to be baptised (Luke 12.50). A torrent of divine judgment fell upon Him in the hours of His sufferings at Calvary; He was immersed in that deluge of wrath. Ignoring the brackets of the verse, the reading would be this; "The like figure whereunto even baptism doth also now save us by the resurrection of Jesus Christ". Whatever aspect of salvation you deem this to be it is linked with the resurrection of Christ, the event that signalled God's satisfaction with the work of the cross. It is His death and resurrection that lays a foundation for salvation, and in the lead up to v.21 Peter had been majoring on these great facts. Baptism is but a picture of these events and in itself could never save. In fact the ritual does not even provide either physical or ceremonial purification, as did certain ablutions in Old Testament times: "not the putting away of the filth of the flesh".

Positively, baptism is "the answer of a good conscience toward God". Conscience is the monitor within us that enables us to discern right from wrong. It is only on the basis of the work of Christ that any man can have a "good conscience". That good conscience demands (the basic meaning of the word "answer") that we take the step of baptism, giving serious thought to the moral and spiritual implications of such a step of obedience, and its declaration of loyalty to Christ. The background of the passage is a recurring theme of Peter's epistle, the persecution of the people of God. Believers under pressure would be able to look back to their baptism as a time when there was a public avowal of commitment to Christ, and would be thus fortified in the face of present harassment.

It has been claimed that there are around 150 New Testament passages that teach that salvation is by faith alone. The fact that one or two hard to be understood verses may *appear* to suggest that baptism is also necessary should not detract from the volume of plain statements that show otherwise.

APPENDIX 3. Acts 2.38; ch.22.16

Again, these are verses that give the appearance that baptism is essential for the remission of sins and cleansing. As has been already stated, many parts of the New Testament teach that salvation is by faith in Christ alone, so these verses cannot contradict that fact. In both cases, the people who were being addressed were folks who had been particularly hostile to Christ. In the first instance, Peter had charged his audience with being guilty of His crucifixion. "Ye have taken, and by wicked hands have crucified and slain" (Acts 2.23). In the other case, Saul of Tarsus had been determined to hound the followers of the Lord to prison and to death. Their sins had been very public sins that demanded the very public act of baptism for it to become apparent to all that remission and cleansing had been accomplished. In Acts ch.2, by their baptism "in the name of Jesus Christ", these Jewish people were publicly dissociating themselves from the great evil that their nation had perpetrated in rejecting and crucifying their Messiah.

Verses of a similar nature are Mark 16.15-16 but comments have been made about them in the body of the booklet.

APPENDIX 4. Children

Those who advocate the baptism of young children use a number of Scriptures to try to support their point of view. It is true that the Lord Jesus said, "Suffer the little children to come unto me" (Mark 10.14), but there is no reference to baptism in the context so this could never be used as a proof text for infant baptism. As with adults, children need to come to Christ in the sense of believing on Him (John 6.35).

It is true that households were baptised, but as has been shown earlier, none of these households contained young children.

Some point to 1 Corinthians 7.14 where the children of a believer are said to be "holy", and infer that to be in a believing family makes all family members safe, with the baptism of the young one being a necessary part of that security. Again, there is no mention of baptism in the context, and the word "holy" carries the basic meaning of being set apart. Children of believers have been set apart only in the sense of being more highly favoured than those reared in an ungodly household. The influence of the believing father or mother affords them the privilege of being exposed to the truth of the Gospel.

There are some who appeal to Acts 2.39 to reinforce their argument; "the promise is unto you, *and to your children*". It seems clear though that the word "children" carries the idea of descendants, just as frequently the word "fathers" means predecessors.

APPENDIX 5. 1 Corinthians 1.13-17

These verses have been used by some to contend that baptism is not nearly so important as we suggest. Does Paul not say, "Christ sent me not to baptize"? It is true that his main function was to preach the Gospel, but as has been noted from the Acts of the Apostles, his converts were baptised. What he is saying here is that he personally baptised only a very few, just as it is recorded of our Lord's ministry that "Jesus himself baptized not, but his disciples" (John 4.2). In this we see the wisdom of both the Lord and His apostle. To claim that the Lord had baptised them could have been for some a matter of pride and prestige. Similarly, some could have gloried in the fact that Paul had baptised them. To avoid such vanity, Paul confined his personal involvement in baptising to a minimum. It was not that he regarded baptism as inconsequential.

APPENDIX 6. "Baptized for the Dead". 1 Corinthians 15.29

Some who see baptism as being necessary for salvation have pointed to this verse as a key plank of their argument. When faced with the fact that the dying thief was in Paradise without baptism, they suggest that someone else was baptised for him, that is, they were baptised for the dead. If that interpretation is rejected, what does the verse mean? If it is not baptism by proxy what is it? The context is crucial. 1 Corinthians 15 is the great chapter of resurrection, and part of Paul's argument is that believers in general and himself in particular were exposed to great dangers on account of their faithfulness to Christ. Persecution and abuse were the order of the day. He speaks of being in jeopardy every hour and dying daily (vv.30-31). What is the point of facing such perils if there is no resurrection? You might as well "eat and drink; for tomorrow we die" (v.32). That is the argument and that is the setting of our phrase, "baptized

Appendix 6. "Baptized for the Dead". 1 Corinthians 15.29

for the dead". Paul seems to be referring to the fact that martyrdom had carried some away, and the ranks of the Christians had been thinned. But these ranks were being filled up by new people, folks who had just come to the faith and had expressed it in baptism. In that sense they were baptised to take the place of the departed martyrs but they in turn were exposing themselves to danger. Paul's argument is that to do so is foolhardy if there is no resurrection, and so his question, "Else what shall they do which are baptized for the dead, if the dead rise not at all?"

Baptism